Florence Nightingale

The Lady of the Lamp

© 2002 White-Thomson Publishing Ltd

Produced by White-Thomson Publishing Ltd
2/3 St Andrew's Place, Lewes, BN7 1UP

Editor: Anna Lee
Cover Design and Inside Design: Tim Mayer
Picture Research: Shelley Noronha – Glass Onion Pictures
Proofreader: Philippa Smith

First Published in Great Britain in 2002 by Hodder
Wayland, an imprint of Hodder Children's Books

This paperback edition published in 2003
Reprinted in 2003

The right of Kay Barnham to be identified as the author of
this Work has been asserted by her in accordance with the
Copyright, Designs and Patents Act 1988.

Titles in this series:
Muhammad Ali: The Greatest
Neil Armstrong: The First Man on the Moon
Fidel Castro: Leader of Cuba's Revolution
Diana: The People's Princess
Bill Gates: Computer Legend
Martin Luther King Jr: Civil Rights Hero
Nelson Mandela: Father of Freedom
Mother Teresa: Saint of the Slums
Pope John Paul II: Pope for the People
Queen Elizabeth II: Monarch of Our Times
The Queen Mother: Grandmother of a Nation
Gandhi: The Peaceful Revolutionary
John Lennon: Voice of a Generation
The Dalai Lama: Peacemaker from Tibet

British Library Cataloguing in Publication Data

Kay Barnham
    Florence Nightingale. – (Famous lives)
    1.Nightingale, Florence, 1820-1910
    2.Nurses – England – Biography – Juvenile Literature
    3.Crimean War, 1853-1856 – Medical care – Great
    Britain – Juvenile Literature
    I.Title II.Lee, Anna
    610.7'3'092

Printed in Hong Kong

ISBN 0 7502 4018 0

Hodder Children's Books
A division of Hodder Headline Limited
338 Euston Road, London NW1 3BH

Picture acknowledgements:
Bridgeman Art Library 4, 25, 27, 28, 30, 41; Forbes
Magazine Collection/Bridgeman Art Library 21;
Philip Gale Fine Art/Bridgeman Art Library 11;
Camera Press 10, 43; Florence Nightingale Museum
22, 26, 36, 39; Fotomas Index 19, 24, 26, 33, 35, 37;
Hodder Wayland 43; Hulton Archive 5, 17, 29, 31;
Impact Photos 42; Mary Evans Picture Library 9,
15, 16, 20, 23, 32, 40; National Trust 8, 38;
Popperfoto 14, 34; Science and Society Picture
Library 6; Wellcome Trust 7, 12, 13.

Contents

The Lady of the Lamp

It is November 1854. In a hospital in Scutari, Turkey, a lamp brightens the darkened ward. A lone figure begins to move from bed to bed. She pauses many times, bending down to place a cool hand on a forehead or to whisper soothing words. The narrow ward stretches into the distance, rows of beds disappearing into the gloom. In every bed there lies a soldier who is desperately ill. Florence Nightingale has time for them all.

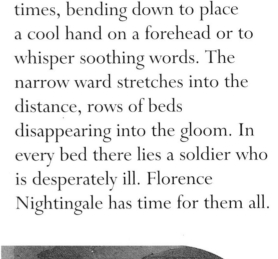

The wounded from the battle-plain,
In dreary hospitals of pain,
The cheerless corridors,
The cold and stony floors.

Lo! in that house of misery
A lady with a lamp I see
Pass through the glimmering gloom,
And flit from room to room.

From *Santa Filomena*, a poem written by Henry Wadsworth Longfellow in 1857, praising Florence Nightingale.

Florence Nightingale became known around the world as the 'Lady of the Lamp'.

Florence Nightingale was the most famous nurse ever. Strong-willed, stubborn and very intelligent, she was determined to make her mark in a world of men.

But it is for her work during the Crimean War that she is best remembered. She led a team of nurses to look after thousands of sick and injured soldiers and then worked tirelessly to improve conditions in hospitals and make nursing the respected profession that it is today.

This photograph of Florence was taken just after she returned from the Crimean War. She was about 36 years old.

Little Rich Girl

Florence Nightingale was born on 12 May 1820 and named after the Italian city of her birth. Her sister Parthenope, known as Parthe, was born a year earlier in nearby Naples. Their parents were very wealthy. Fanny and William Nightingale owned two country houses in England and their European honeymoon lasted for over two years.

The city of Florence, Italy, where Florence Nightingale was born.

Embley Park in Hampshire, England, where Florence spent most of her childhood.

Fanny Nightingale loved to enjoy herself. She was funny and charming, never happier than when she was surrounded by friends. Florence's father, William, was much more serious. He had attended Cambridge University and knew the importance of a good education. He took charge of Florence and Parthe's lessons, teaching them French, German, Latin, Greek, history and philosophy.

Florence was clever and did well at her studies, but her sister had little interest in learning. She would much rather have been visiting friends. After all, what use was learning to a rich girl in the nineteenth century? She knew that she would never have to work and earn her living.

'... the world is put back by the death of everyone who has to sacrifice... his or her peculiar gifts (which were meant... for the improvement of the world).'
Florence Nightingale, 1852.

7

A Call from God

When Florence was sixteen, her life changed. On 7 February 1837 she wrote in her diary that she received a message from God, asking her to help him. Florence was stunned — and confused. What did God want her to do? She waited for more advice but heard nothing. It seemed that she would just have to work it out for herself.

Florence's sister, Parthenope, is believed to have painted this picture of Florence as a young woman.

Florence and her family had a wonderful time during their travels in Europe, seeing the sights and mixing with other wealthy people.

Later that year, Florence and her family set off for Europe. This was no ordinary holiday. Florence's father wanted to teach his daughters more about the world by showing them the marvellous things in it. The Nightingale family travelled from France to Italy and on to Switzerland, visiting beautiful cities on the way. They went to the opera, admired the work of famous artists, and attended lavish dinners and balls.

Then, in Switzerland, Florence saw dreadful poverty. Her bubble of enjoyment burst at once. This was a side to life that she had never seen before. Was this her mission – to help the poor?

'It was pleasant to wake up in Florence… to fling wide the windows… to lean out into sunshine with beautiful hills and trees and marble churches opposite.' From *A Room With A View* by E.M. Forster, a novel about British tourists in Italy in the nineteenth century.

Women in Victorian England

In nineteenth-century England, women's lives were mapped out for them. If they were poor they worked long hours, often in dreadful conditions, to earn enough money to survive. If they were rich they were expected to marry, have children and run a household. Careers were left to men.

As Florence saw it, she had the choice of being trapped in a marriage or trapped in a life of reading, music and embroidery. She'd been educated to a very high standard – was she to have no opportunity to use her education? Apart from helping the poor each summer holiday, Florence felt that nothing she did was worthwhile. She was miserable and soon became ill.

Women miners in Lancashire. During the nineteenth century women often had to work in dangerous and difficult jobs.

An upper-class Victorian dinner party. The thought of becoming a genteel Victorian lady drove Florence to despair.

In an attempt to help her recover, Florence was sent to stay with her Aunt Mai in London. There she discovered mathematics. Her family wasn't pleased about this – at the time maths wasn't a subject that women studied. But Florence continued learning despite her parents' disapproval. Her knowledge of maths was to prove very useful indeed.

'Women never have a half-hour in all their lives... that they can call their own... Why do people sit up so late, or... get up so early? Not because the day is not long enough, but because they have no time in the day to themselves.'
Florence Nightingale, 1852.

Kaiserswerth Hospital School

At the age of 24, Florence Nightingale realized that she wanted to devote her life to nursing. But nursing was not a respectable job, especially for someone with Florence's background. Hospitals were filthy, cramped, badly run and full of male doctors and patients. Unmarried, rich young ladies were not allowed to spend time alone with men. Worse still, nurses had a reputation for being drunken, lazy and open to bribes. It took Florence a year to pluck up the courage to ask her mother and father if she could become a nurse. The answer was 'no'.

'For the sick it is important to have the best.' Florence Nightingale in February 1855.

A nineteeth-century cartoon of a grumpy nurse. Nursing wasn't considered a respectable profession at this time.

Despite writing to hospitals to find out more about them, Florence became depressed. A trip to Rome failed to lift her spirits and two offers of marriage just made her more miserable. She turned them down. How could a married woman ever become a nurse?

Two long years later, returning from a trip to Egypt, Florence came across a hospital school in Germany. This time her mind was made up. She must go there to study nursing! And six months later, in July 1851 and against her family's wishes, she did.

The hospital and training school at Kaiserswerth, Germany, where Florence first learned about nursing.

Working in Harley Street

Florence's stay at Kaiserswerth in Germany was all too short. She was eager to continue nursing on her return to England but had to take care of an unexpected patient – her father. William Nightingale now began to understand just how much his daughter wanted to be a nurse. He decided to support her.

Meanwhile, Parthe's health was beginning to worry everyone. When she and Florence were together, Parthe suffered from worsening fits of hysteria. One of Queen Victoria's top doctors

Florence and her sister Parthenope. They did not bring out the best in each other.

14

suggested that Florence and her sister should spend time apart. This was a blessing in disguise. Away from her family, Florence had much more valuable free time. She gathered vast amounts of information from hospitals and used her maths skills to record the facts and figures about patients and illnesses in a clear and logical way.

Then Florence's dream came true. A superintendent was desperately needed to organize and manage the Institute for the Care of Sick Gentlewomen in Harley Street, London. Florence was given the job. Her mother and sister were appalled. Unable to stand the arguments, her father moved out.

'We are a breed of ducks who have hatched a wild swan.'
Fanny Nightingale, Florence's mother.

Florence was overjoyed to start work in Harley Street.

The Crimean War

In March 1854 the Crimean War began. It was to be
a glorious war and the British Army was given a grand
send-off. Everyone was sure that Russia would be beaten
quickly and that Britain would triumph as it always did.
But the army was poorly organized and those in charge
made mistakes that would cost thousands of lives.

The British Army's first error was their choice of camp, in
the middle of an area well known for the deadly disease
cholera. Troops were soon dying.

'It is with feelings of surprise and anger that the public will learn that no sufficient preparations have been made for the care of the wounded... there is not even linen to make bandages...' William Howard Russell in *The Times* newspaper on 30 September 1854.

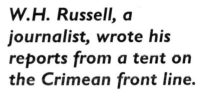

W.H. Russell, a journalist, wrote his reports from a tent on the Crimean front line.

Next, it became clear that there weren't enough ships to carry the soldiers from Scutari across the Black Sea to the Crimean Peninsula. To make room, medical equipment and supplies were left behind. When they landed, the British troops were weakened by disease and the tiring journey. Those who survived the fighting were shipped back to Scutari.

In England, the awful conditions in the Crimea were reported in *The Times*, shocking the public deeply.

When Russia invaded the Balkans, Britain, France and Turkey declared war on Russia, fighting against them on the Crimean Peninsula. The Battle of Inkerman (see page 21) took place in November 1854.

17

Arrival in Scutari

By now, one of Florence's greatest friends, Sidney Herbert, was Secretary of War. He knew that Florence was the ideal person to organize the hospital in Scutari, which held many of the sick and injured. He wrote at once, asking her to take a group of nurses to the Crimea. Florence was overjoyed. This was God's work, at last!

Florence Nightingale was made Superintendent of the Female Nursing Establishment of the English General Hospitals in Turkey. This time her entire family supported her. She and a group of thirty-eight nurses set off on the tiring journey to the Crimea, arriving in Scutari on 4 November 1854.

Below left *A map of Europe during the 1850s.*
Below *A map of the region in which the Crimean War was fought.*

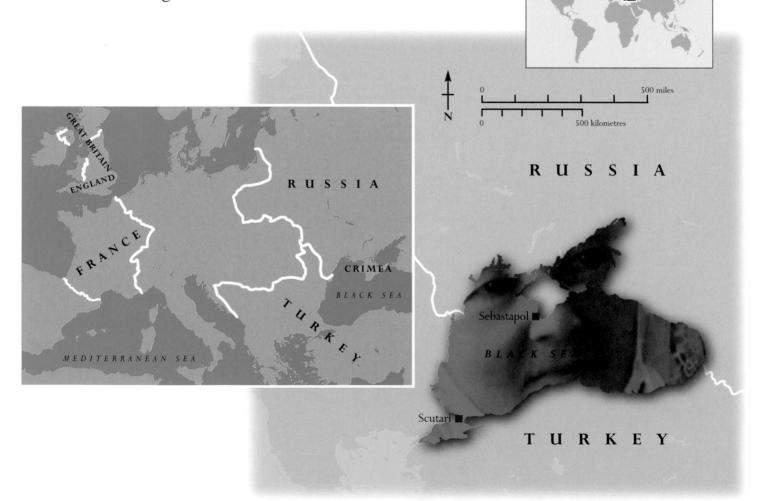

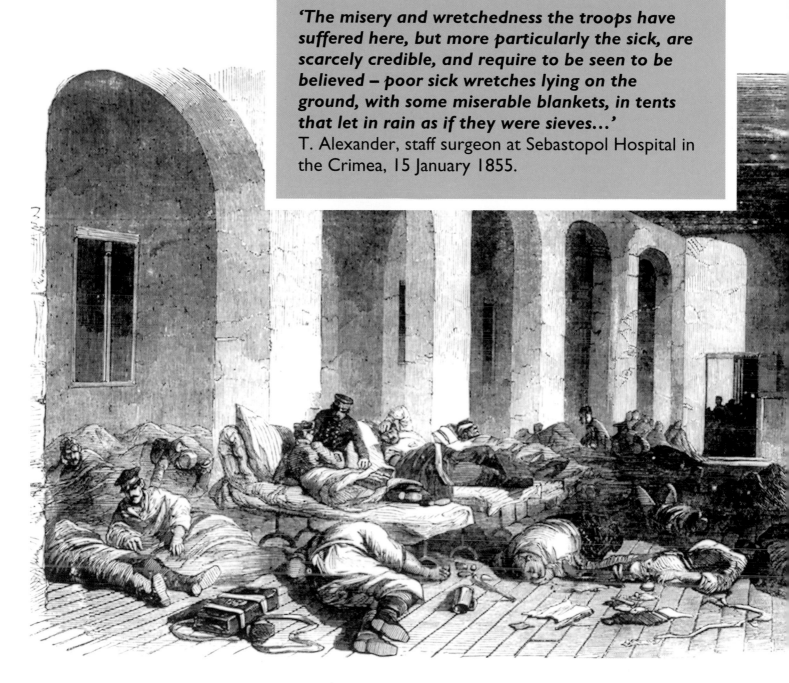

'The misery and wretchedness the troops have suffered here, but more particularly the sick, are scarcely credible, and require to be seen to be believed – poor sick wretches lying on the ground, with some miserable blankets, in tents that let in rain as if they were sieves...'
T. Alexander, staff surgeon at Sebastopol Hospital in the Crimea, 15 January 1855.

Even though she'd heard of the appalling conditions on the battlefields and in the hospitals, Florence still found it hard to believe the living hell she found. Thousands of patients were crowded into filthy, rat-infested corridors. Mountains of paperwork meant that vital supplies were held up. The conditions were so bad that soldiers who survived injury then had to battle disease.

A ward at Scutari would have looked similar to this picture of a ward in the Russian hospital during the Crimean War. Both hospitals were crawling with rats, cockroaches and lice.

Florence and the Doctors

Florence was eager to start work but she ran into difficulties almost immediately. The army medical staff complained that they hadn't been told of Florence's arrival and refused to let her take charge. An army hospital was no place for women!

So Florence waited. If she annoyed the doctors they would see to it that she was sent straight home. She had made it this far — she couldn't fail now. Florence told her nurses that they must not help unless they were asked to. So they worked in the kitchens, doing their best to make sure that patients received healthy food. And they waited.

Florence paid for many of the supplies at Scutari herself. She knew how important it was for her patients to eat and drink properly.

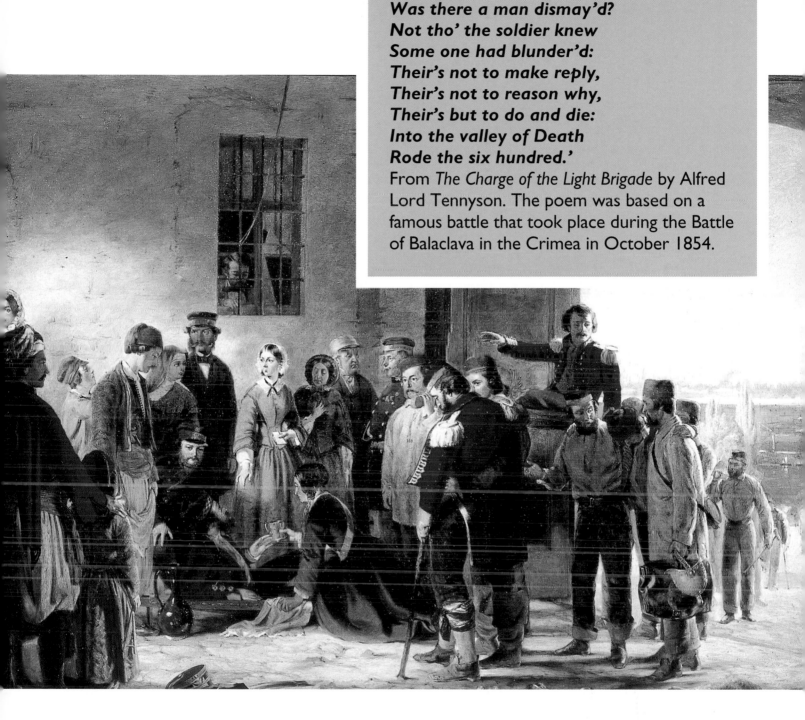

After the Charge of the Light Brigade, Scutari was flooded with yet more wounded soldiers.

More and more sick, injured and dying arrived from the battles of Balaclava and Inkerman. By the end of November, those in charge could refuse Florence's help no longer. She took over at once, using the knowledge she had gathered in the past to try and bring order to the filthy, diseased chaos in Scutari.

The Long Winter

Despite Florence's hard work, disease and infection were still claiming lives at Scutari, while sick and injured soldiers continued to pour into the hospital. An epidemic broke out in December 1854 – all at once, patients and members of staff became ill. Many died. No one could work out why this was happening. There had been lots of improvements in the hospital. Patients were well fed. They were clean. So why did they keep on dying?

'In all our corridors, I think we have not an average of three limbs [arms and legs] per man.'
Florence Nightingale on the number of patients in Scutari Hospital who had lost limbs.

The wards of Scutari hospital were so infected that soldiers had a better chance of survival on the battlefields.

In March 1855, an investigation into the high death rate solved the mystery. Scutari hospital was built on top of old, rotting sewers. This was infecting both the water supply and the wards themselves. The sewers were immediately cleared out and the wards ventilated to allow in fresh air. The death rate soon began to fall.

Scutari hospital and the nearby cemetery were both full to overflowing.

Florence now worked even harder, turning her attention to the battlefields. But while visiting Balaclava she became gravely ill with a mystery illness. After two weeks Florence recovered, but was very weak. Aunt Mai came from England to care for her.

Mary Seacole

Florence Nightingale was not the only nurse capable of organizing hospitals in the Crimea. As Florence became better known, another nurse who struggled to help the British troops was all but ignored. Mary Seacole, a Jamaican 'doctress' and expert in tropical diseases had treated British Army soldiers in Jamaica during the 1840s. She also worked in Panama and Nicaragua before travelling to England in September 1854. Over the years she had treated many cases of cholera and become a respected nurse. Mary volunteered to go to the Crimea and was turned down by Sidney Herbert's wife – because of her race.

But Mary Seacole refused to give up so easily. She travelled to the Crimea using her own money, setting up a hospital in Balaclava near the battlefields. She was on the scene to help treat and care for the soldiers as they were injured, or fell ill, saving many lives.

*In 1857, Mary Seacole told her story in **The Wonderful Adventures of Mary Seacole in Many Lands.***

Many nurses worked with Mary Seacole on the battlefields of the Crimea. This nurse is giving a wounded soldier a drink.

Despite all her good work, Mary Seacole was penniless and unknown by the end of the war. At last, in 1867, Queen Victoria supported a new Seacole Fund, to thank Mary for her good work in the Crimea.

The End of the War

Florence Nightingale had now become a celebrity. The public couldn't get enough of her, buying ornaments, postcards and paintings of the lady with the lamp. Then a collection was begun. The idea was to buy something to thank Florence for her dedication and hard work. But public support was so strong and so much money was collected that the Nightingale Fund was set up instead. Florence's mother wrote to her daughter to say how proud she was – a great change from her original thoughts about Florence's career.

While Florence was in the Crimea, and after her return, newspapers and magazines featured articles about her work. Here she is shown as the nightingale bird.

*'A lady with a lamp shall stand
In the great history of the land,
A noble type of good,
Heroic womanhood.'*

From *Santa Filomena*, a poem written by Henry Wadsworth Longfellow in 1857, praising Florence Nightingale.

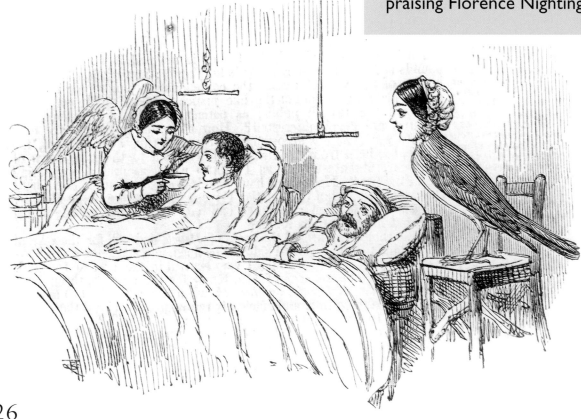

Ornaments of Florence stood on many Victorian mantelpieces.

By the end of the war, thousands of British and Russians had lost their lives. These sailors were burying one of the many dead.

But in Scutari Florence wasn't popular with everyone. She was adored by her patients but the Chief of Medical Staff didn't feel the same way. He accused her of lying and disobeying orders. Florence fought back and was proved innocent. Then, in March 1856, she was made General Superintendent of the Female Nursing Establishment of the military hospitals of the Army.

In April 1856 the war ended. Britain was victorious and, in July of that year, Florence left Scutari and went home.

Florence and Queen Victoria

What did the future hold for the world's most famous nurse? She dreaded the thought of the cheering crowds that awaited her in England. Florence Nightingale had spent almost two years surrounded by disease and death in the Crimea. Rest was all she wanted. She travelled back to England secretly, avoiding parties, parades and civic receptions. Now she had to decide what to do next.

After she returned home in 1856, Florence couldn't forget what she had seen in the Crimea.

A painting of Queen Victoria in 1859. When Queen Victoria and Prince Albert met Florence Nightingale in September 1856, they were moved by her determination. 'I wish we had her at the War Office,' said Queen Victoria.

'Oh my poor men who endured so patiently. I feel I have been such a bad mother to you to come home and leave you lying in your Crimean grave. 73 per cent in eight regiments died during six months from disease alone – who thinks of that now?'
Florence Nightingale, 1856.

Florence realized that she couldn't forget the soldiers who had died in the Crimea. Something had to be done to prevent death on such a large scale ever happening again. In her new role as General Superintendent she was determined to make army hospitals safer places to be treated.

When Queen Victoria and Prince Albert sent an invitation asking to meet her, Florence jumped at the chance. Here was the perfect opportunity to air her views on the Crimea, to convince the queen and her husband that conditions in army hospitals needed to be improved. The British royals were very impressed with her words.

The Royal Commission

In 1856, with Queen Victoria's support, the Royal Commission was set up to look into the state of army hospitals. Its aim was to prevent so many unnecessary deaths in the army. Sidney Herbert was made chairman of this official government enquiry. As a woman Florence couldn't take part in the investigation, but she could gather information and evidence for male politicians.

Florence didn't just assist the commission, she wrote her own report about the army's hospitals. Before the war she had always thought that personal cleanliness was the key to good health. She had been shocked by the discovery that it was the conditions at Scutari hospital that had caused so many deaths.

Soldiers at a military camp in Aldershot. Even during peacetime, many soldiers died from the unhygienic conditions in the army.

Lord Sidney Herbert, a close friend of Florence and chairman of the Royal Commission.

Florence's many statistics backed up her report. She knew how many had died in the Crimea – as well as when and why they had died. Worse was to come. Florence discovered that even during peacetime, the death rate in the army was twice as high as that of the civilian population. She blamed unhygienic conditions in army barracks and hospitals, poor diet and disease.

The Royal Commission and Florence Nightingale's report had positive results. The death rate in the British Army dropped.

'...the good sense, the unalterable patience, the heroic simplicity of our men will never be an old story.' Florence Nightingale in a letter accompanying her report given to the War Office.

Notes on Nursing

Working day and night on her report, Florence had paid little attention to her health. Three months after it was finished she collapsed, becoming so ill that everyone thought she would die. She did get better, but remained very frail and never fully recovered her strength.

However, ill health was no obstacle to a woman like Florence Nightingale. She was now freer than she'd ever been before – free to do exactly as she wished. If she didn't want to see someone she would ask her staff to say that she was ill. Florence's mother Fanny and sister Parthe were very rarely invited to her bedside.

Lea Hurst, the house where Florence stayed after her return from the Crimea.

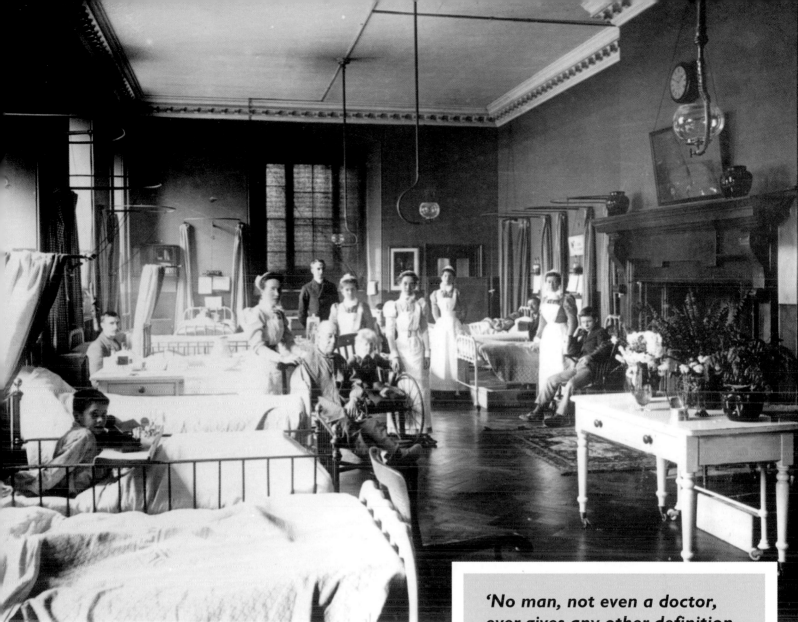

Florence's book, Notes on Nursing, **suggested ways to make the hospital ward a more pleasant place to be.**

'No man, not even a doctor, ever gives any other definition of what a nurse should be than this – 'devoted and obedient'. This definition would do just as well for a porter. It might even do for a horse.'
Florence Nightingale, 1859.

Florence continued with her work – without interruptions. She wrote *Notes on Hospitals*, which described how hospitals could be improved. There should be more space around each bed and hygiene should be of the utmost importance. Next, she turned her attention to nursing itself, writing her most famous book – *Notes on Nursing*.

St Thomas's Hospital

Florence Nightingale's opinion was highly valued and she was kept busy answering letters from all round the world. After *Notes on Hospitals* was published in 1859, she was asked many questions about hospitals – how they should be run and how they should be built. St Thomas's Hospital in London was among those that wanted advice on the design of a new hospital building. Remembering the Nightingale Fund, it dawned on Florence that the new St Thomas's Hospital would be the ideal home for her new nursing school.

There were many heated discussions over where the new hospital should be built. Florence was in favour of open land, but the governors of the hospital decided upon a site near the Thames.

'It may seem a strange principle to enunciate as the very first requirement in a hospital that it should do the sick no harm.' Florence Nightingale, 1859.

St Thomas's Hospital at the end of the nineteenth century. The foundation stone was laid by Queen Victoria in 1868.

Florence had much more say on the design of the hospital.
Wards would be hygienic and well ventilated and large
windows would allow light to flood in. They would be
pleasant places for both staff and patients to be.

*St Thomas's Hospital
became the home for
the Nightingale
Training School.*

The Nightingale Nurses

In 1860 the Nightingale School for Nurses was founded. Sarah Wardroper, formerly the Matron at St Thomas's Hospital, became head of the school, but Florence kept a close eye on the trainee nurses.

Florence with some of the nurses at the training school. She checked all the trainee nurses' reports.

The Nightingale School was the first non-religious training school for nurses and it was different in other ways, too. Only the best nurses were given a place. Nurses went to lectures but learnt most of their skills on the bright, airy wards, treating real patients.

And they were not only taught to look after the sick, they were also trained to teach others in hospitals around the world. By 1890, Nightingale nurses had been sent to teach in Germany, Sweden, Canada and the USA.

During her lifetime, Florence Nightingale did a great deal to give nursing a good name. She made it easier for women to become nurses (at this time, nursing was not thought to be suitable for men) and showed the public that nursing was an important job.

All trainee nurses were provided with a uniform, as well as meals and accommodation.

'*The School of Nursing stands supreme among her magnificent achievements.*' Historian Adelaide Nutting, speaking in 1939.

37

Florence's Health

Since her time in the Crimea, Florence had never been well. She suffered from a mystery illness that may have been brucellosis (an infection caused by bacteria) or possibly post-traumatic stress disorder (caused by the trauma of the Crimea). She was bedridden for much of her life, but used the time to continue with her work – uninterrupted. She also liked to visit her sister Parthe; they now got on well.

Sidney Herbert was Florence's public voice. Through Sidney, Florence advised the government on matters linked with public health and sanitation. When Sidney resigned because of health reasons in 1861 Florence was furious. How dare he let her down when there was so much still to be done? She wrote him an angry letter, making it clear that she was frustrated and upset. It was a letter that Florence was to regret two months later, when Sidney Herbert died.

Florence's room at Parthenope's home, Claydon House. Florence often continued with her work while visiting her sister.

Florence missed her friend immensely but her work went on. She continued to give the government advice, campaigning for the improvement of public health for the rest of her life.

'Her brain cut... into the core of things.'
Adelaide Nutting, 1939.

Florence in her later years. Although she was often bedridden, she kept in touch with friends by mail.

Hard Times

Florence Nightingale supported many causes. She was deeply worried about the awful conditions in workhouses, home to the very poorest people who couldn't afford to look after themselves. In return for hard work, the poor, the orphaned and the mentally and physically disabled were fed and given food and lodgings. But they were grim, dirty and miserable places to live. Florence put pressure on the government and, in 1867, the Metropolitan Poor Act was passed to reform workhouse conditions.

Life in workhouses followed a strict and often harsh routine. These men are eating their dinner.

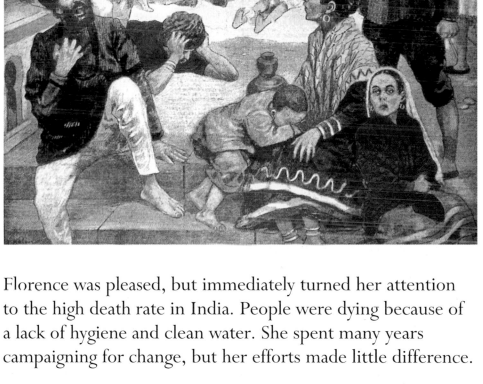

> '*I am sure that you bid me God speed in all my objects: the training of Nurses... the sanitary reform in our Army and country generally: the sanitary development – and above all the "irrigation development", to prevent famines of India: poor millions of our starving fellow subjects.*' Florence Nightingale.

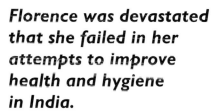

Florence was devastated that she failed in her attempts to improve health and hygiene in India.

Florence was pleased, but immediately turned her attention to the high death rate in India. People were dying because of a lack of hygiene and clean water. She spent many years campaigning for change, but her efforts made little difference.

Then, tragedy struck in 1874 – her father died. Now Florence was responsible for caring for her difficult family. But her mother and sister had changed. They no longer criticized her but instead asked for her advice. The Nightingale family had finally found peace.

A Legend Dies

Despite Florence's increasing age and the loss of her sight in 1901– the year that Queen Victoria died – she worked until the age of 86. She was now very frail and unaware of much that went on around her.

But she was still remembered by the public, the government and the monarchy. In 1907 King Edward VII, Queen Victoria's son, gave Florence Nightingale the Order of Merit. It was the first time a woman had received the award.

King Edward VII, who presented Florence with the Order of Merit.

'Among my treasured memories is that of a visit to her early in the present [twentieth] century. One forgot the invalid and saw only the aged and beautiful face, the unfaded keen eyes, the cheerful smile, the eager listener. One noted most the surprisingly strong full voice, and I hear it still saying "Goodbye, come again".' Adelaide Nutting, 1939.

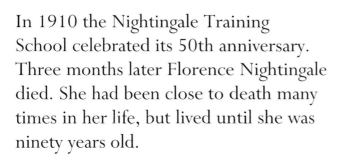

In 1910 the Nightingale Training School celebrated its 50th anniversary. Three months later Florence Nightingale died. She had been close to death many times in her life, but lived until she was ninety years old.

In her will, Florence asked for a quiet funeral and to be laid beside her family at Embley. Her wishes were followed, but although Florence had tried to avoid fame throughout her life, she could do nothing about it now. Her memorial service at St Paul's Cathedral in London was attended by thousands and thousands of the nurses that she had inspired.

This statue of Florence stands in Waterloo Place in London. It commemorates the wonderful work Florence did in nursing.

Florence Nightingale's Legacy

The Nightingale Foundation holds an annual service to commemorate the life of Florence Nightingale and celebrate the nursing profession. Over 2,000 nurses and health workers attend every year. During the service, a lamp is passed from one nurse to another – symbolizing the knowledge that is passed from nurse to nurse.

Thanks to Florence Nightingale, nursing is now a highly respected profession.

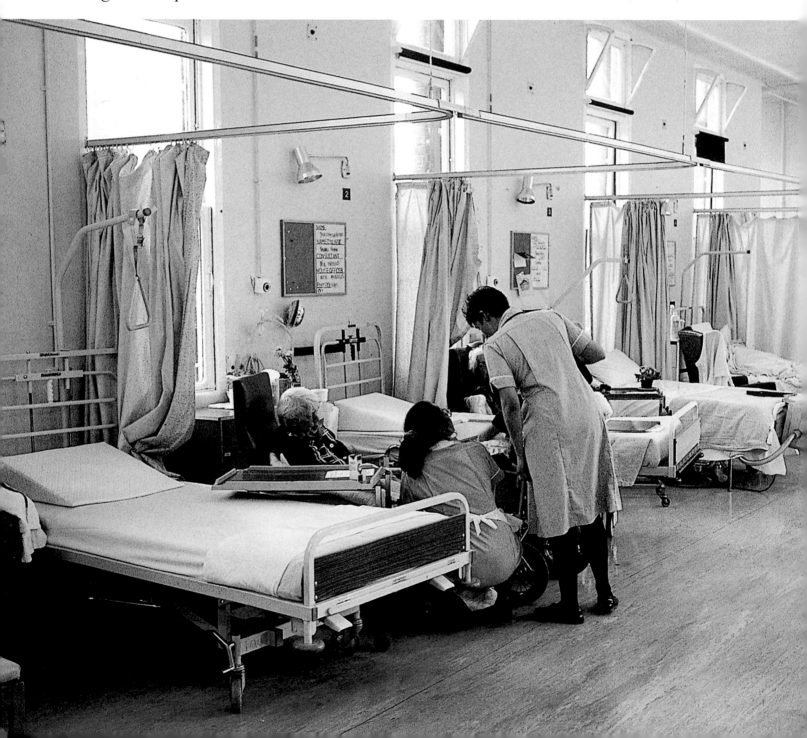

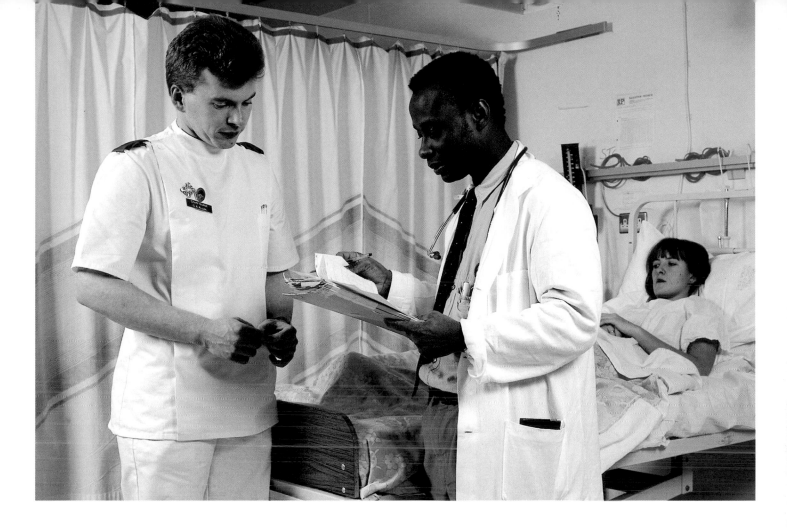

Today, both men and women train to become nurses.

Florence Nightingale was not the only reformer of the nursing profession, nor was she the world's best nurse. But her two years in the Crimea brought nursing to the attention of the public and showed that women could be strong and determined. And although she is best remembered for the role she played in Scutari, she spent the rest of her life working tirelessly to improve nursing, hospitals and public health. Her time in the Crimea showed her the importance of hygiene and she campaigned endlessly to make sure that everyone benefited from this knowledge.

> *'When I am no longer even a memory, just a name, I hope my voice may perpetuate [keep alive] the great work of my life. God bless my dear old comrades of Balaclava and bring them safe to shore.'* A transcription of a recording of Florence Nightingale made in 1896.

Glossary

Bacteria Tiny germs that may cause disease.

Cholera An often fatal disease that is caught through infected water supplies. Symptoms include severe vomiting and diarrhoea.

Dysentery A severe infection that causes diarrhoea.

Epidemic When a lot of people catch one disease at the same time. Today, flu epidemics sometimes happen in wintertime.

Hysteria Wild and emotional over-excitement.

Lecture An educational talk to a group of people.

Monarch The head of a royal family.

Orphaned When a child loses both his/her parents.

Philosophy The study of ways of thinking.

Profession A career.

Sanitation Conditions that help the public stay healthy.

Statistics A large group of numbers that can be used to prove something.

Superintendent A person in charge of an organisation.

Symbolize To stand for.

Trauma An upsetting and disturbing experience.

Typhoid Severe infection that causes a rash and stomach pains.

Ventilated When air is allowed to enter and leave a room.

Further Information

Books to read
For younger readers:
Stories from History: Don't Say No to Flo! by Stewart Ross (Hodder Wayland, 2002)
Beginning History: The Life of Florence Nightingale by Liz Gogerly (Hodder Wayland, 2003)

For older readers:
Notes on Nursing by Florence Nightingale (Dover Publications, 1970)

Sources
Florence Nightingale by Pam Brown (Exley Publications Ltd, 1988)

Florence Nightingale and the Crimea: 1854-55 edited by Tim Coates (The Stationery Office, 2000)
Museum Resource Pack (Florence Nightingale Museum, 2001)

Place to visit
Florence Nightingale Museum
2 Lambeth Palace Road, London, SE1 7EW
Tel: 020 7620 0374

Websites
Website: http://www.florence-nightingale.co.uk

Date Chart

1820, 12 May Florence Nightingale is born in Florence, Italy.

1837, 7 February Hears God asking for her help.

1837, September Travels with her family to Europe.

1839, April Returns from Europe.

1844 Turns down Henry Nicholson's proposal of marriage.

1847 Meets Sidney Herbert.

1849 Turns down Richard Monckton-Milnes' proposal of marriage.

1851, July Starts her training at Kaiserswerth.

1853, April Becomes Superintendent of the Institute for the Care of Sick Gentlewomen.

1854, March Britain, France and Turkey officially declare war on Russia.

1854, 25 October The Battle of Balaclava takes place.

1854, 4 November Florence and her thirty-eight nurses arrive at Scutari.

1854, 5 November The Battle of Inkerman takes place.

1855, 10 May Becomes seriously ill while visiting the battlefields at Balaclava.

1856, 29 April The Crimean War is over.

1856, 28 July Florence Nightingale leaves Scutari.

1856, September Meets Queen Victoria.

1856, November Moves to a hotel in London to asssist the Royal Commission.

1857 Turns down Sir Harry Verney's proposal of marriage.

1858 Sir Harry Verney marries Florence's sister Parthenope.

1859 *Notes on Hospitals* and *Notes on Nursing* are published.

1860, 24 June The Nightingale Training School opens.

1861, 2 August Sidney Herbert dies.

1865, October Moves to her own house in Mayfair, London.

1874, 10 January Her father dies.

1880, 2 February Her mother dies.

1883 Awarded the Royal Red Cross.

1890, May Parthenope dies.

1890 Her voice is recorded by the Edison Company.

1907 Awarded the Order of Merit.

1910, 13 August Florence Nightingale dies in London.

Index

All numbers in **bold** refer to pictures as well as text.